DARE TO BE INFLUENTIAL

MAXIMIZING YOUR **POSITIVE INFLUENCE** WHILE STILL **BEING TRUE** TO YOU

LISA REHUREK

INDIE BOOKS
INTERNATIONAL®

No part of this publication may be reproduced or distributed in any form or any means without the prior permission of the publisher. Requests for permission should be directed to permissions@indiebooksintl.com, or mailed to Permissions, Indie Books International, 2424 Vista Way, Suite 316, Oceanside, CA 92054.

Neither the publisher nor the author is engaged in rendering legal or other professional services through this book. If expert assistance is required, the services of appropriate professionals should be sought. The publisher and the author shall have neither liability nor responsibility to any person or entity with respect to any loss or damage caused directly or indirectly by the information in this publication.

Maximize Your Influence Process™ is a pending trademark of Lisa Rehurek.

RFP Success® is a registered trademark of Lisa Rehurek.

ISBN 13: 978-1-952233-31-9
Library of Congress Control Number: 2020921749

Designed by Joni McPherson, mcphersongraphics.com

INDIE BOOKS INTERNATIONAL, INC®
2424 VISTA WAY, SUITE 316
OCEANSIDE, CA 92054

www.indiebooksintl.com

DEDICATION

To anyone who strives to be a positive influence in the world.

CONTENTS

CONTENTS

DARE TO BE INFLUENTIAL

CHAPTER 1

Why Becoming Influential Is Important

"I'm sorry, the computer made an error.
You're not influential, you have influenza."

Consider this classic example of positive influence.

Mega movie star Marilyn Monroe had become an avid fan of the African American jazz singer Ella Fitzgerald back in the 1950s. Fitzgerald wasn't particularly well-known and was playing at small, low-key venues. After Monroe saw Fitzgerald perform for the first time, the two become fast friends.

Through that friendship, Monroe learned Fitzgerald was unable to land a gig at a famous West Hollywood nightclub because the owner felt Fitzgerald was too heavyset to draw crowds. Yet Fitzgerald longed for this opportunity because she knew it would change the trajectory of her career.

In 1955, Monroe, a top-ten box office star at the time, used her influence to persuade the owner of the nightclub to book Fitzgerald. The blonde bombshell was a publicity magnet and promised to sit in the front of the house every night and bring along guest celebrities and the media.

The agreement was made, Fitzgerald's shows sold out, and that did indeed change the trajectory of her career. Fitzgerald, who went on to win fourteen Grammys and be dubbed the "Queen of Jazz," never had to play in crummy small venues again thanks to Monroe's positive influence.

The World Needs More Positive Influencers

The world is calling you. You do not need to be a celebrity to have impact and influence. But to be truly influential, you do need to discover your own genuine path.

You are surrounded by people who influence you every day. Some reflect positivity; however, there are many who flood the universe with negativity. We are influenced by people in the limelight: politicians, actors, musicians, podcasters, celebrities, and authors. And the list goes on and on. The less obvious, however, are the everyday people around us.

No doubt, you remember parental warnings about bad influences. When you were growing up, did your parents ever tell you, "Don't hang out with so-and-so; they're a bad influence"? Perhaps you relate to the Jimmy Buffett song, "We Are The People Our Parents Warned Us About."

When we are young, we struggle to find the direction the rest of our lives will take. We look to role models, whether they are friends, family members, or famous people. Speaking of bad company, I personally got into plenty of trouble as a young teenager trying to find my voice and my place and allowed myself to be influenced by the wrong people. You'll get to hear a few of those stories along the way.

What Negative Influence Looks Like

In a 2013 CouponCodes4u.com survey, more than 2,400 parents from all over the country were asked which famous figures were the *worst* role models. Miley Cyrus was at the top of that list, with 68 percent of the vote. Justin Bieber and Chris Brown were on that list, too. All clear examples of negative influence. Also, all examples of young stars who were, themselves, trying to find their voice and their place. And that showed up in negative ways.

As we get older, we start to learn more about ourselves and what we are willing to tolerate. Yet it is still easy to be swayed by others' influence—both positive and negative.

Positive Influence Is A Choice

Being influential is not just reserved for people with authority or fame. We all get to choose to be a positive or negative influence, and to what degree.

We influence people daily, whether we are aware of that or not. The level of influence depends on the roles we play and the amount of visibility we have.

––––––––––––

The more visible you are, the greater the responsibility for positive influence.

––––––––––––

If you are in a leadership role, if you want to be in a leadership role, or to be a leader in any way, being influential is part of the gig.

According to the Center for Creative Leadership, the ability to influence is one of the four core leadership skills needed in every role. In fact, read any article on effective leadership, and you will read about the importance of influence.

Ken Blanchard, author of *The One Minute Manager*, says: "The key to successful leadership today is influence, not authority." Dale Carnegie wrote a whole book on *How to Win Friends and*

Influence People, which talks about the role that influence plays on getting things done. That book sold over thirty million copies and is one of the best-selling books of all time.

Being influential gives you the freedom to drive change, lead a vision, and inspire others; all things we need in today's world.

The thing is, you do not just wake up and all of a sudden own the influence label. Furthermore, you do not become influential just because someone gave you a leadership title. In fact, many people with authority are not great at being influential because they have never done the work required to become a successful leader.

Busting The Influence Myths

Some believe you are either influential or you are not, and they contend that influence is not something that can be learned. Others raise the concern that attempting to be influential and persuasive are code words for being manipulative and controlling.

These are common misperceptions. Dismissing the power of positive influence is a gross miscalculation.

Influence is not something you are born with; it is a learned skill. Sure, you may be naturally likable and approachable— pieces of the influential puzzle—but there is so much more to it.

Influence can be learned. But it is an intangible quality that is all about the strength of your presence. You must be willing to put in the hard work and the time to grow into that role. It takes consistency, practice, and humility.

Influence is not manipulation. Unfortunately, there are a small handful of people who use their influence for bad. You are not one of them.

Influence is about allowing for a win-win scenario. It cannot be forced; people are naturally drawn to people they choose to be influenced by. What that tells us is influential people have magnetism; they have presence.

_____

True influence has staying power; it is more than just a one-time sugar high.

_____

One example is Peyton Manning, believed to be one of the greatest NFL quarterbacks of all time. He has an impressive list of accomplishments and accolades, including two-time Super Bowl Champ, Super Bowl MVP, five-time NFL MVP, and fourteen-time Pro Bowler.

As an athlete, he is impressive. But his success has come from more than just his on-field talent. His ability to positively influence his teammates, his fans, and the cities in which he has played made him a better quarterback. He has carried himself with grace and modesty on and off the field, both in his words and in his actions. He knew he had to build the foundation of trust to influence from his genuine self.

The Responsibility Of Positive Influence

Developing yourself as a genuine influential leader is powerful. With it comes great responsibility— responsibility for creating good in the world, for inspiring other sincere leaders, and standing in the light when you are scared s***less. Leading the charge instead of letting others influence you into being something or someone you are not is hard and scary. It requires courage and determination.

Everyone has the potential to be a positive influence. There is groundwork that needs to be laid to develop yourself into a positive influential leader. In the coming chapters, you will learn the base principles to help you develop this groundwork.

DARE TO BE INFLUENTIAL

CHAPTER 1:
Why Becoming Influential Is Important

1. Choose to be a positive influence.

2. Discover your own genuine path.

3. Use your influence to help others.

4. Think in terms of win-win scenarios.

CHAPTER 2

Six Ways To Be Influential And Still Be Yourself

FOLLOW YOUR DREAMS!

©Glasbergen
GLASBERGEN

"It's supposed to inspire, but most employees see it as permission to take a nap."

"The ability to influence people without irritating them is the most profitable skill you can learn," said Napoleon Hill, author of the 1937 mega-bestselling book, *Think And Grow Rich*.

To be influential means having the power to cause an effect on people in indirect or intangible ways.

To produce these intangible effects requires many things. Among them: good communication, taking appropriate action, and valuing others.

But there are hidden secrets that most people do not talk about. This book will introduce you to the six hidden secrets that will increase your level of influence.

This is not about becoming someone else to become influential—this is about becoming the best version of you.

While these six hidden secrets are powerful in your influencing journey, it is important to understand that there is no one-size-fits-all path when it comes to influencing. You need to discover for yourself that *you* are a leader with influence.

You must consciously and consistently choose to develop your influencing skills. And then, when you put them into practice, it must come from your heart. If you are not sincere, if you try to fake it, people will see right through you.

There are six hidden secrets outlined in this book to help you develop your genuine influential self.

My methodology is called the *Maximize Your Influence Process*. These secrets are built on the foundation of being true to yourself and to guide you into building that influence from a place of sincerity.

The six hidden secrets of my Maximize Your Influence Process are:

1. Screw expectations!

2. Know you, do you

3. Conquer your emotions

4. Kick the yes-men to the curb

5. Ditch the excuses

6. Quit whining and work hard

In the next part of the book, we are going to take a deep dive into each of these secrets.

My Rocky Road To Influence

Before we go into that deep dive, let me tell you a bit more about why I am the person sharing these secrets with you.

I have always been someone who pushes the limits, as far back as I can remember, even as a kid. I have this *perfect* sister who always followed the rules and rarely got into any trouble. I was always the one pushing the limits, getting sent to my room, getting grounded, and even getting my mouth washed out with soap.

I have one specific memory when a friend got a new playset in his backyard. My sister and I were so excited to go play on it. When we got there, they were making up rules about how we were going to play on it: my friend first because it was his, my sister second because she was older, and I would go last.

I remember we lined up and had to wait for our turn based on these completely arbitrary and ridiculous rules that I had no part in setting. Needless to say, I wasn't too happy about that, so I decided I would protest by biting my sister on the arm. And I bit her so hard that it broke the skin, which of course, caused me to receive serious punishment. It might not surprise you to know I have many stories like this.

My restless, non-rule-following ways have trailed me throughout my life and were never more obvious than in school. I was not ever interested in the academic side of school. I found it boring and boxed-in, but I managed to squeak through and graduate high school.

Then I went to college and struggled. In the first two years after high school, I went to four different colleges and dropped out each time. My father happened to be president at one of those colleges, so you can imagine how that went over with him.

I had so many majors. I am not sure I can even count them all. I started with drafting (I wanted to be an architect), then moved on to criminal justice, then to math, creative writing, archaeology, court reporting, and I'm sure there were more in there that I can't even remember.

All of this once again on the heels of my sister, who graduated in under four years with a change of major, a change of schools, and on the dean's list. I just could not seem to find my place, and I thought there was something wrong with me because I was not like her.

I finally thought I found my place in college once I discovered the right major: one that did not keep me sitting in a boring classroom full-time. My major: hotel and restaurant management. It was perfect because it was diverse, challenging, fun, and *way* outside the box. It was a brand-new offering at my college, and back then, there were not a lot of colleges around the nation that even offered this program.

The bouncing-around trend continued after graduation, but I did spend some time in the hotel/restaurant field.

- I co-ran a restaurant in Door County, Wisconsin, but that was just seasonal.

- Then, on to Wendy's as an assistant manager, but it was too greasy and structured.

- Next was Quality Inn and a few other hotels, but they became too rigid.

- I tried working at a bank, but the job was boring.

- I worked at an insurance company doing data entry (what was I thinking there?).

- A construction company job lasted a few weeks, but there was not enough work to keep me challenged.

Of course, all this time, my sister was doing her thing. She got a finance degree, went into banking, and she has had only a handful of employers in the thirty years since.

It took me a while, but I came to realize that the bouncing around was not because I was unstable, or I could not figure things out. I bounced around because who I am at my core does not fit into those traditional jobs, into the same boxes that most everyone else tries to fit.

Eventually, I fell into a great and unexpected opportunity with a company that allowed me to be my out-of-the-box self. They let me build, create, fix, and then move on to the next thing. In other words, they let me figure stuff out. And it was great for eleven years until I landed a new role that boxed me in.

It was then that I left to venture into the world of business ownership, first as a partner in several businesses, and eventually into my own business.

Even at the onset of business ownership, I struggled because I did not know who I was as a business owner. I did not own my strengths and my values, and I was trying to do things according to the direction provided by mentors and gurus that did not fit my narrative. This was when I discovered these six ways to become influential and put them into play, and it has been a shot out of a cannon ever since.

I am blessed that while I did not love learning in an academic environment, I am a lifelong learner. I observe, I read, and I do a lot of inner work. I have learned that working toward someone else's vision is not where I was meant to be. Heck, it is not where anyone is meant to be unless their joint vision is well matched.

We all are free to create our own destiny. For me, it is that box full of holes and bent corners from my rolling around and pushing the limits in creating and building new things. When I am in those types of positions, I am naturally influential.

People are drawn to those who can stand in their truth.

Being grounded in who I am has given me the opportunity to be influential in some circles and not in others. People are not one-size-fits-all, and neither is leadership. Each one of us should be poised to create our own circle of influence, right where we genuinely belong. It will not be for everyone, but it will be exactly where we are supposed to be.

DARE TO BE INFLUENTIAL

CHAPTER 2:
Six Ways To Be Influential And Still Be Yourself

1. Screw expectations

2. Know you, do you

3. Conquer your emotions

4. Kick the yes-men to the curb

5. Ditch the excuses

6. Quit whining and work hard

CHAPTER 3

Screw Expectations!

"IF YOU'RE NOT ABSOLUTELY THRILLED AND DELIGHTED WITH OUR PRODUCT, CALL US TOLL-FREE AND WE'LL BE HAPPY TO HELP YOU ESTABLISH MORE REASONABLE EXPECTATIONS."

Stephanie was shocked the day I told her she needed to screw expectations.

Stephanie (true story, but details changed to protect confidentiality) wanted to strategize how to approach a Request for Proposal (RFP) her company was bidding on, and this is exactly what my company does. She cared passionately about doing high-quality work for her clients. In fact, clients often complimented her firm on its innovative approaches to problem-solving.

Stephanie and her team were great at the technical part of an RFP but realized they were lacking in making a persuasive case for their solutions. Their undeserved misfortune was they invested so much time and energy in gaining technical acumen, little time was left to learn the art of RFP persuasion. That is when she asked to talk to me.

"What I care deeply about is making sure the technical information is correct," said Stephanie. "However, our batting average is unfairly low. What do we need to do to win this and unseat the incumbent?"

"You need to screw expectations and take risks," I said. "They are expecting the same old boring but technically proficient response that everyone else will provide. You can't bore them into buying."

Stephanie took a deep breath and sighed.

"How risky?" asked Stephanie.

"The riskiest path is the one you are on," I replied. "Keep doing what you are doing, and you will fail."

Stephanie did not like hearing that.

"Look, Stephanie, if you want to win, you are going to need to be provocative," I said. "You can't do the same thing they expect if you want to unseat a solid incumbent. You need to smack them between the eyes to make them think twice."

"I don't know if I can pull that off," said Stephanie.

"I'm not saying it is going to be easy," I replied. "But you can do it, and I am here to help you succeed."

Stephanie and her team took our recommendations to do something unexpected. They pushed the limits on how they addressed their response, being bold and brazen in asking questions to guide the reviewers into a different way of thinking. Indeed, it was a leap outside of their comfort zone.

The good news: the strategy worked. By screwing the expectations, they defeated the incumbent to win the bid.

Life Is Full Of Expectations

Everyone has expectations that they put on themselves, expectations from family and friends, societal expectations, professional expectations, the list goes on. There are probably all sorts of thoughts coming to life in your head right now, aren't there? Some of these expectations are conscious, but many are unconscious.

Following what everyone else wants for us or what we think we *should* do is detrimental to our success. The truth is, it is time to bust through those beliefs and stand in the power of who we are and who we want to be. Being yourself is the ultimate way to positively influence, from a position of self-awareness and self-belief.

I am direct and don't sugar coat a lot. That is why this chapter is called "Screw Expectations." It is the perfect title to stand in my power and let others know who I am and the message I want to convey. It is okay to ignore other people's expectations of you; throw caution to the wind and be true to you.

Now, I am not telling you to go out and rob a bank or do something unethical. Heck, I have this odd desire to steal a backhoe and go for a joyride, but that does not mean I'm going to do it.

Finding your own path, doing things that will make you happy is the most important thing you can do.

When we constantly pay too much attention to what everyone wants and expects from us, we are living life to gain the approval of others. Plain and simple. And how that shows up in business is that your feet will not be planted solidly on the ground. You will waver because you will not remember things. You will confuse yourself, and that leads to accepting a leadership style that has been chosen by others and forced onto you, with its accompanying forced viewpoints.

You cannot influence from a place of force.

And when you do not know who you are, or what you truly stand for, you will be forcing agendas, communication, and viewpoints onto others from a less-than-authentic position.

You have heard the adage: Lead by example. If you do not know who you are, if you are not following your heart's path, people will not follow because there is no way to set a genuine example.

There must be authenticity for true positive influence to be present.

How I Learned To Screw Expectations

Unconsciously I have studied expectations my entire life. I placed a lot of expectations on myself based on what I thought family and society wanted for me. There was not necessarily anyone looking over my shoulder, constantly saying, "This is what you have to do." Sure, I had family that expected that I do certain things, but the expectations were out of love and desire for me to have a fulfilling life.

The journey I took to find out what I wanted was vastly different than what my family and society would expect from me. I came from a steady, stable family. My dad was an educator, my mother a nurse. Their careers were stable, and my sister followed suit. It is what you did—graduate from high school, go to college, get a good job where you save up for retirement, get married, have children, retire comfortably. Sounds like a lovely life for many people. Not for me.

As I mentioned, I dropped out of several colleges. On top of that, I changed my major so many times I cannot count them all. But it was because I had absolutely no idea what I wanted. Looking back, I was constantly fighting against societal expectations while still trying to make people happy.

That was a challenging proposition. I finally went back to college and got my bachelor's degree at age twenty-four, but I majored in hotel and restaurant management, which was also somewhat "beyond expectations" at that time. I did not stay in that industry long, and I moved around in jobs until I landed a corporate role that allowed me some freedom to discover my value. I remember my grandmother saying to me, "It's so nice that your sister is still working in her chosen field." Gut. Punch.

Frankly, I have no idea if that was meant to be a dig at me, but it sure felt like it at the time. I believed I was doing something wrong by not continuing in my degreed field. Heck, there was a lot I felt I was doing wrong. I did not start saving for retirement when I was supposed to; I got divorced, which back then was not nearly as common as it is now, and there was a lot of societal judgment. I realized I did not want children, which is still somewhat controversial in some societal circles. I discovered that living a "normal" life was not what I wanted for myself. The only thing that mattered to me is what I wanted my life to *feel* like and what ultimate mark I wanted to make on the world. Once I figured that out, it allowed all those other expectations to fall away.

Because my life was not working the way it was supposed to, I always felt in conflict within myself. Life was hard. Now, let me give the caveat that my life has been beautifully blessed and happy. But there was always something missing because I was spending so much time and energy in conflict with what seemed to be expected of me.

I was fighting uphill because I was not following my path.

I thought if you're in a great, loving relationship, the next step is to get married, and so I did; you go to college to get a great job so you can retire comfortably, which I did.

Yes, I now know I hurt people in the end because I made choices that were not in alignment with what I wanted. There was a very forceful power in me that refused to accept anything less than my true calling that was pulling continuously against the expectations of those closest to me. I was in constant conflict. Even when it came to success, I was always thinking about meeting other people's expectations as part of my own success: past mentors, family members, even people I had yet to meet influenced my decisions. I would focus on whether this is something they would do, or they would approve of, or they would notice me for. Certainly, these thoughts still creep into my head today because it is very much human nature.

But now, my decisions are no longer based on those thoughts. Even if they creep in, I recognize them and squash them like a bug. Because I was able to finally stand in my own power of the person who I wanted to be, at age forty-five, I completely reinvented my career. I found fulfillment not only professionally but also personally because I stopped fighting it.

Evidence Supports Screwing Expectations

Influencing others takes the guts to stand up for who you are and to stop worrying (or whining!) about what everybody else thinks. It takes courage to be the one in the front of the room, influencing others. It is not easy because people judge. It is far easier to stand in the back of the crowd, stay internally focused, and not let anyone know who you are. But easy is not the path for everyone. If you are reading this, my guess is you do not want easy; you want to influence, and you are feeling called to do so.

A question asked in an October 2018 *Psychology Today* article titled "Live Your Life for You, Not to Please Expectations" by Gustavo Razzetti really brings this home. "Do you sometimes feel like you don't love your life? Like, deep inside, something is missing?"[1] According to Razzetti, this happens when we are living someone else's life and allowing other people to influence or determine our choices.

Another important point that the author shares is that people will have multiple hopes for you, and social pressure fluctuates. Can you imagine the energy it takes to keep up with that? It is exhausting. I know because I lived with these pressures for an exceptionally long time, and it *is* frustrating.

In the aforementioned article, Razzetti said: "Frustration is the gap between what people expect from you and who you are." Do you want to live in frustration?

I have always found it odd that we strive to live our lives based on someone else's expectations. Most people do not live the life that they want because they are so caught up in trying to do it right according to someone else's definition. I remember when I was working a corporate job, I would constantly hear people say they hated their job. "This is just a job, a means to an end."

I never logically understood that because my pragmatic mind knew there was a simple solution. Get another job, plain and simple. But, of course, I *did* understand it because I had lived it. Luckily, the dreamer in me *needed* more, so I always kept pushing to find more. I was never satisfied with the status quo. I wanted to experience fulfillment (there is that word again!) from what I did. I still hear that comment to this day, people constantly complaining about how much they hate their job. Follow your dreams, people! Not to be cliché, but life is too damn short.

The George Clooney movie, *Up in the Air*, has one of my all-time favorite movie lines. To set the stage, Clooney's character is a corporate downsizer. During one downsizing conversation, the terminated employee is visibly upset that he is losing his job. He is angry, defensive, and annoyed. There is a lot of fear because he cannot see what is next for him. Clooney's character calmly says:

> *"Do you know why kids love athletes? Kids love athletes because they follow their dreams. How much did they first pay you to give up on your dreams? And when were you going to stop and come back and do what makes you happy?"*

Whew. That is a heavy question. When are *you* going to come back and do what makes you happy? You want to influence? That is the key.

If you hate your job, if you are not fulfilled, if you are just going through the motions, people feel your negative energy. You do not even have to open your mouth as it is seeping out of every pore of your being. No one is drawn to that energy.

People who stand in their own power and have self-confidence are natural magnets. They have underlying natural energy that makes people want to be around them. That cannot be faked. No one is inspired by a negative Nelly.

Peter Economy, known as "The Leadership Guy," shared in an article in Inc.com that the most important habit for becoming the most influential person in the room is believing in yourself.[2] It is your character that plays a key role in your being influential.

DARE TO BE INFLUENTIAL

CHAPTER 3:
Screw Expectations!

So how, you ask, do you get to the point of letting go of what everyone else thinks to stand in your own power? From my experience, here are some key steps you want to take. I suggest taking out a journal or notebook and jotting down your thoughts. These are not one-and-done exercises; they should continue to evolve over time.

1. Ask yourself this question: *What is the most important feeling I want and need in my life?* I am not talking about the "haves," I am talking about the *feeling.* What do you want to feel each day when you wake up? For me, I want to feel fulfilled. Once you know this, do not allow yourself to settle for anything less than that feeling.

2. Learn as much as you can about yourself. Self-awareness is an underdeveloped skill for many of us, but it is where all the

power lies. Take talent assessments, read a variety of books on self-development, ask trusted advisors. And above all else, be honest with yourself about what you are allowing because you want it, versus what you are allowing others to control.

3. Write down your core values. What do you stand for, and what will you not compromise on? The more you get clear here, the less and less you will be willing to compromise on the most important things. And that is powerful.

4. Make a list of all the expectations you have in your life—your own, your family's, your friends', society's. Do this over the course of several weeks because you will not be conscious of them all right out of the gate. Then spend some time with each one of those expectations, breaking them down to rid yourself of the ones that do not serve you.

5. Decide what you want to be known for. Since this is a business book, focus

on what you want to be known for professionally. Many people call this your legacy, but that word does not resonate with me since I did not have children. But one thing I know for sure, I want people to remember me for inspiring others to follow their own path and screw the expectations of others.

6. Write down your fears. What are you afraid will happen if you eliminate each of those expectations? What will happen if you do not follow the "expectation rules"? What if you make choices that allow you to experience personal fulfillment?

7. Learn to trust. Trust in yourself; trust in whatever higher power/universe you believe in. In reality, you are the only one that can do you and who knows you. No one can argue about the true you; you just must be in tune with who that is. Trust that you ultimately know and that you just must learn to listen. Trust that the true you is exactly who you are supposed to be. Trust allows you to let

go of ego and judgments. If you are an ultimate people-pleaser, this concept is going to be hardest for you. Trust will be the most important component. Trusting in yourself, but also trusting that the better you know you, the more available you will be to share your true self with others. Radiating the inner confidence in your truth will be much more influential than sharing any wrongly focused version of you.

CHAPTER 4

Know You, Do You

"I used to hibernate for four months of the year, but then a motivational speaker made me realize this was a form of self-sabotage that was keeping me from making the most of my potential."

There was silence on the other end of the phone. I paused, waiting for a reaction.

He was still there. Perhaps he was a bit choked up, maybe overwhelmed by the information I had just shared.

"Tell me what you're feeling right now," I asked.

More silence. Then Jason tried to speak, but his voice was shaky. He cleared his throat.

"We can take a five-minute break if you'd like," I said.

"No, I'm good," replied Jason.

Jason and I had just spent the past hour pouring over the results of a recent talent assessment he had taken.

Quietly, he said: "This wasn't what I expected."

I asked him to tell me more.

"I think you just changed my life," he said.

Jason was a sales intern at a large manufacturing firm. Sales was in his blood. His father was a salesperson, his brother was a salesperson, and so was his grandfather and two of his uncles. Jason grew up believing that he was destined for a career in sales.

Yet here he was, in what he thought was the internship of his dreams, but he was struggling.

Jason did not see success. He was a senior in college, and even college had been a struggle for him. He hated school, he was miserable selling, and he felt like a complete failure.

At the beginning of the call, Jason shared something with me. "Sales is all I've ever known," he said. "But what if sales isn't for me? What then? I don't know anything else."

With college graduation impending, Jason was freaked out.

Jason's company was allowing all employees to take a scientific talent assessment that measures behaviors, motivators, and acumen. Jason decided he might as well take advantage of the offer and see what it was all about. He could never have imagined that it would lead to a conversation that brought a completely new understanding of his ability to sell.

I gave Jason two pieces of information that led to his breakthrough.

First, I told him that he was well-suited for a job in sales, but he needed to focus on the right type of sales role. He was wired to build long-term relationships, with the ability to cultivate those relationships over time. He was a farmer, a salesperson oriented toward sustaining and growing an established customer base by upgrading existing and upselling new products. However, he was being groomed for a hunter-style transactional sales role that required cold-calling, networking, and research to find new clients, which was stressing him out.

Second, I asked him if he liked school. His answer was an emphatic, "No!"

"What don't you like about it?" I asked.

He said he struggled to pay attention in class, he did not get good grades, and he could not retain the information.

"That's because you aren't motivated by learning the traditional way," I said.

Jason is motivated to learn by doing, by touching and feeling, and by getting his hands dirty. In essence, an on-the-job form of learning.

These two pieces of information allowed Jason to understand things about who he was that defied the expectations he had placed on himself (there is that word *expectation* again). He had been on the path that was right for others, but that was not *his* path.

Armed with this information, Jason now had the ability to stay true to who he is at his core. And in doing that, he was able to move forward with excitement and a vision for his future. If he stays true to who he is, he will find the success he craves.

You Are Much More Influential As Your True Self

Let us face it, finding our way in this world is not always easy. Letting go of expectations is hard, ignoring what other people around you are doing is hard, and not wanting what someone else has is hard.

One of the most powerful things you can do for your ultimate well-being is to get to know *you*. Sounds a little corny, sure. You may even be wondering, *how can we not know who we are?* That is fair. What happens is that we get influenced by outside voices. In our quest to find success, or to become the person we want to become, we look to others for guidance. That is natural, and it is certainly valid. The challenge is it is easy to get lost. It is easy to get caught up in the emulation of others.

There will always be someone there to tell you that you are doing it wrong, thinking incorrectly, or moving in a bad direction. When you are not grounded in who you are, these commentaries will derail you. And that's when your potential to positively influence others will crumble. When you try to please everyone, you please no one, including yourself.

You may not realize it, but we all influence every day of our lives, whether we are aware or not. People are watching, especially in today's world. We influence in positive ways, yes, but also in negative ways. This book is for those who want to be more aware and dare to be a positive influence even when you do not think people are watching.

When we see someone powerful fall from grace, it is generally because they have not been showing up in their whole, true self. They are trying to be someone they are not, and it catches up with them.

I am certainly not saying that we do not have to adapt. Adapting is part of life. What I am saying is that we need to know who we are to truly adapt and flex when and where needed. There is a big difference between adapting and faking.

Truly knowing who we are allows us to adapt with grace, purpose, and power.

Here is what happens when you do not truly know yourself:

- You will struggle to set boundaries

- You will spend a lot of energy trying to hide your weaknesses

- Fear and stress will run rampant

- You will not be able to regulate your emotions

- You will constantly be defensive

- People will see right through you; thus, you lose credibility

- You will turn people off

- You will not trust yourself

Have you ever had a conversation with someone and all they do is talk about themselves? Usually boasting, and they never take a breath to look you in the eyes and ask about you and your needs? This person sorely lacks self-awareness.

A fellow business owner recently reached out to me and asked for a meeting so he could learn more about my business. I took him up on his offer, but during our face-to-face meeting, he never asked me about my business. He talked non-stop about all his accomplishments, how fantastic he was, and how great he was at connecting people.

At one point in the conversation, he said, "I am here to tell you, I have a lot more experience in this area than you do."

Hmm. Interesting comment considering this person did not know me at all. Not one to be shy, I shot back the following question: "I'm interested to hear how you know you have more experience in this area than I do?"

He just stared at me. And to his credit, after a few seconds, he lowered his shoulders, sighed a deep sigh, and then kind of laughed and said, "Wow, you're right. I don't actually know your experience in that area."

Of course, he did not choose to then ask me anything about my experience; he just continued down his blubbering path.

This is an unaware person. You could call it ego, or narcissism, or any other negative word. But in a nutshell, he is not aware of himself enough to be able to regulate his thoughts or refocus the conversation to include another person's participation.

I knew from our initial exchange that he wanted to bring me into his networking organization. He was attempting to sell me, which is a form of influence. But his approach had zero credibility.

It would not at all surprise me to know this person feels unsettled in who he is. He likely feels like a fraud, and I am here to tell you, he came across as a fraud.

No one wants to emulate a fraud.

Eventually, people will see through the fakery. To truly be influential, we must get out of our heads and into our hearts.

People are drawn to what is in your heart, but not always to what is in your head.

Do you have the guts to listen to your heart?

It seems strange that we would be fearful of being ourselves. Somehow, we do not know that trying to be someone we are not results in the thing we are most fearful of—that people will recognize our faults.

When you know yourself, you will have an innate trust in yourself. You will be able to trust your word, your direction, and your abilities.

So, ask yourself:

What do you want? What do *you* want?

What do you believe? What do *you* believe?

The honest and real answers to these questions have the power to change your life.

When I Was A Fish Out Of Water

When I was twenty-one, I thought I wanted to work in the hotel industry. Coming out of college with a hotel and restaurant management degree, I floundered around in multiple hospitality jobs. I gave up and went to school to become a court reporter, but I never finished. I was lost.

Then one day, I received a call from a woman I had previously worked for, who said her husband was looking for some help in his growing company.

The job was with an actuarial consulting firm. And at the outset, I thought nothing could be more boring.

For the first few years, I was like a fish out of water. Sitting in boardrooms with actuaries, health policy consultants, and CPAs, it was hard to see where I fit.

It became a joke one year after the leadership team took an online personality profile assessment and learned that I was one of two Peacocks (optimistic, spontaneous, usually found in sales and marketing of new ideas) in a sea of Owls (methodical, detail-oriented, often engineers and accountants). By that time, I had learned to embrace that I had value to add to this group: an inquisitive personality open to considering alternatives and exploring change as opposed to one focused on facts and details, a trait that is fundamental to the success of the Owls.

That occurred because of a fantastic mentor, Steve, who saw something in me that I could not see in myself at the time. He encouraged me to ask questions, as dumb as they may have seemed. He taught me how to ask smart questions but to speak up and not be shy.

Perfect, I thought. Speaking up and not being shy was right in my wheelhouse.

I remember sitting in meetings, wanting to ask a question, and being scared to death to ask it for fear of sounding dumb. The first few times I decided to go for it, I remember a pause and a few blank stares. It felt like a lifetime, although it was probably only a few seconds. And in those moments, I would usually get an answer like this:

"Actually, I have no idea. Great question."

What? I thought to myself. How could these smart people not know the answer?

As in any situation, the subject matter experts are so much further beyond the public in their industry-specific knowledge that they cannot see the forest for the trees. I became acutely aware that by being open to exploring new ideas and processes, I added value to the team. I learned how to ask simple yet smart questions and became a sought-after internal resource because of it.

That job ended up being my longest corporate job, and the last company I worked for before becoming a business owner. Those eleven years and six roles were fantastic learning experiences for me in so many ways.

By far, the biggest growth experience for me was learning to recognize my own value.

The aftermath: To this day, that company and many of its consultants are clients of mine. They saw value in what I offered, and I was able to build substantial credibility and influence over the years. That trust has never been erased, and those Owls now seek out this Peacock as a much-valued resource.

The moral of the story is this: we all have value; you must find yourself to learn what your value is.

It goes beyond external value. Understanding and knowing your internal value system is also imperative. If you don't have your flag planted solidly in your value system, you will get uprooted and blown away.

How I Almost Got Derailed

I left my corporate career because I was afforded a fantastic opportunity to start a business with an ex-colleague. At the time, it felt like the absolute perfect opportunity for me. I had been in a boxed-in role in my current company, and I was searching for my next step. It felt like a silver-platter, low-risk opportunity.

About a year into my foray into business ownership, my partner and I formed a second partnership with another company. We were doing some online selling that had me a little uncomfortable. It wasn't anything illegal, but to me, it was unethical.

My main business partner had been someone for whom I had a high level of respect. At the time, I trusted his judgment, but there was this little voice in the back of my head that kept nagging at me. Something didn't feel right.

One day, the partners came to me and asked me to sign my name to the merchant accounts. If you know anything about merchant accounts, once you get blacklisted, you're in big trouble. They needed me because they all had already been blacklisted.

This was a defining moment because I knew if I didn't sign, I would be seen as not being a team player. But my integrity and my value system were screaming at me.

In the end, I chose not to sign. I'll be honest: that was the beginning of the end of that business partnership. I went on to have my personal integrity tested several more times, and ultimately, I chose to walk away. At the time, it felt heavy. I wasn't sure what I was going to do next. And ultimately, I walked away from a future sale that would have netted me a lot of money.

But knowing myself, that's not how I wanted to make money.

I don't have one single regret. I can still hold my head high and feel immensely proud of how I handled what became a toxic environment. I was tempted, I was challenged, but I stayed the course because I knew who I was and what I was not willing to compromise.

It seems, oftentimes, we hold on because we are afraid to see what's on the other end. We compromise our values and our integrity because of the people that we're dealing with that maybe we trusted in the past, or we think they're bigger and better than us. Nobody can be bigger and better than standing in our own integrity.

Evidence Supports That Being Yourself Leads To Success

Influence comes from confidence, credibility, and courage. And you cannot get to any of those if you are not self-aware. Knowing who you are, what you stand for, and the *why* behind it all is imperative.

The Leadership Guy, Peter Economy, addressed a quote by Oprah Winfrey in a February 2018 Inc.com article.[3]

The quote, "I consider it a compliment that I am full of myself," could easily garner some criticism as having been narcissistic. And let us face it, there are many people who think that's exactly what Oprah is.

But in truth, what Oprah meant was that she is at her absolute best when she is not afraid to honor herself. In honoring herself, she can receive respect and step into her power. And even Oprah acknowledges this takes some work. You must want it.

Oprah also mentions you must work on the "alignment of your personality—your gifts that you have to give—with the real reason why you're here." In fact, many in the personal development field would wholeheartedly agree.

Self-awareness is a powerful tool. It takes courage to search the depths of our selves. You must set ego aside and be open to exploration. It takes continuous learning and opening yourself up to exploring your weaknesses just as much as your strengths.

TTI Success Insights, an industry-leading assessment provider dedicated to revealing human potential through assessment solutions and research, does loads of research on this topic. They state by understanding your own strengths and weaknesses, you can pivot weaknesses into opportunities. Instead of trying to hide your weaknesses, or be in fear of them, own them.

If you think other people cannot see your weaknesses, you are kidding yourself. We spend so much time trying to "hide" the things we think make us look weak, ugly, or incompetent. But make no mistake, the world can see us, often much clearer than we can see ourselves.

Strengthen Your Confidence In You

Have you ever heard the phrase, "Steer into the skid"? It is a reference to driving, but metaphorically it means steering into the unknown or the negative.

Steer into the weakness skid; you will be a lot happier.

Once you get back into alignment and continue moving forward toward your destination, you can claim a small personal victory. You have bolstered confidence in your skills and reinforced your ability to avoid potential calamity—you can begin to trust your ability to choose wisely. You can plant your feet solidly on the ground because, with each new success, you are growing and claiming the power of your true self. You will begin to correct your path by conquering your fears; you will possess new confidence going forward that you will make good choices leading to positive outcomes. Other people's expectations will no longer unduly sway you; criticism will no longer own you, and your ability to positively influence others will skyrocket.

DARE TO BE INFLUENTIAL

CHAPTER 4:
Know You, Do You

The journey to self-awareness takes moxie. Not everyone is willing to dig deep, stay the course, and grow into the best version of themselves. When they are successful, we see the tried-and-true influential leaders take the field and play to win.

Do you dare to play in this league?

If the answer is yes, keep going.

There are ten questions to which you must be willing to say yes. You might not yet be ready to say yes to them all, but *you must want to work toward the yes*. If you desire it, you will make it happen.

Take some time to sit with each of these questions. Ponder what a "yes" or a "no" will mean for each one. It's even more powerful if you journal about each one.

For some, you may not know what a "yes" or a "no" would look like right now. That's okay. Work that out over time by observing others showcasing that trait and journaling about the experience. To use a cliché statement: This is a marathon, not a sprint; do the work at the pace that is right for you.

1. Are you willing to be uncomfortable?

2. Are you ready to work through your fears?

3. Are you inclined to set ego aside?

4. Are you open to learning how to address your emotions?

5. Are you able to admit (and own!) your shortcomings?

6. Are you willing to stand in your true self, even if it is not the popular stance?

7. Are you eager to own the space of being influential in a positive way?

8. Are you ready for this life-long journey?

9. Do you have the guts to listen to your heart?

10. Are you willing to commit to steering into the weakness skid?

CHAPTER 5

Conquer Your Emotions

"Of course you have a purpose in life. You pay taxes, don't you?"

Sylvia, the escrow officer, was having a rough day. We were meeting for the signing of my first solo mortgage. To say I was excited is an understatement. Not only was Sylvia late, but when she finally arrived, she was not the pillar of pleasantness.

Without any eye contact, Sylvia tossed a pen to me across the table. There was not much of an introduction, just straight to the signing. She would toss me each signature page and abruptly tell me to sign "at the bottom."

This went on for about ten minutes. At that point, I had had enough.

Not being someone to stay quiet, I put my pen down, looked her in the eyes, and asked her, "Should we reschedule this appointment? You seem to be having a bad day."

For the first time, Sylvia looked directly at me. She did not speak for about ten seconds. I could see her lip quivering and tears welling up. I also noticed her body language was slowly changing into a more relaxed position.

"I am so sorry," she finally blurted. She went on to tell me about all the events of the day that had contributed to her sour mood.

At that moment, Sylvia had built up anger and resentment because of outside factors in her day. Not only had she allowed these outside activities to negatively influence her, but she was also projecting her emotional response on to me.

Sylvia was trying so hard to hold in her emotions; she had over-compensated. She did not have any awareness of how her emotions were possibly affecting people around her.

I had a choice in this situation—let her influence me with her negativity and send me into a bad mood for the rest of the day, or stay the happy course and bring her along for the ride.

The funny thing is after we had a good laugh about the situation, Sylvia joined me at happy hour to celebrate this milestone. I'll take that as a win.

The moral of the story is this: We all have a choice. We can allow other people to subconsciously influence us for good or bad. Or we can conquer our emotions so we can choose how we are influenced and how we will positively influence others.

Conquering Our Emotions

We have all heard the phrase, "Emotional Intelligence" or EI. It is become a bit of a buzz phrase, and rightfully so because it is such an important aspect of our success, our ability to influence, and our credibility.

So, what exactly *is* Emotional Intelligence?

There are a million different definitions, but I'm partial to this simple definition by MindTools: "Emotional Intelligence is the ability to recognize your emotions, understand what they're telling you, and realize how your emotions affect people around you."

But what does it mean in our day-to-day lives? And why is it so important?

Leaders with high EI understand their own feelings, what they mean, and how their emotional response can affect other people.

Your emotional intelligence impacts most everything you do and say each day. It is not something we're born with; it's something we must learn to develop. The most influential leaders have learned this secret to success.

EI affects how we:

- manage behavior
- navigate social complexities
- make personal decisions
- manage stress
- communicate

The inability to manage these will, without question, impede your ability to influence. If you want to better influence, learn to develop your EI.

Let us look deeper at the correlation between EI and influence.

First, emotional responses kill credibility. Now, before you start sending hate mail, this is not to say you should not have emotions. That is not at all what we're talking about. It is about managing your emotions in relation to the situation. When you are interacting with others, your ability to stay calm, listen, and rationally process an event puts you in a position of authority. People take notice.

When was the last time you positively responded to someone who was yelling or showcasing a high level of stress? Likely never. People are naturally drawn to a poised leader.

Second, emotionally intelligent people do not lead with ego. The emotion behind the ego is fear. When you can regulate your fear, you can manage your ego.

It does not mean ego and fear don't exist; it means they don't control the outcome.

One of the greatest gifts you can give yourself is the understanding that it is okay for people to think and feel differently than you. If the ego is in the way, you will never be open to allow for the personal growth that comes with a willingness to consider other people's opinions and feelings.

Lastly, being emotionally intelligent allows you to stay fully true to you without letting emotions derail or persuade you. Remember, you want to be in the influence driver's seat, not the backseat observer.

Conquering your emotions means having the ability to recognize the emotion but move out of it quickly. Instead of letting one event ruin your entire day, spend five minutes working through it, and move on. With high EI, you can work through the hard times quickly.

Think about a time when you were driving down the road, and a car cut you off, and they reached out the window and flipped you off. Now, you have a choice—are you going to react with your emotions by following their lead and flipping them off in return? Well, sure, maybe sometimes. I may (or may not) have done that a time or two.

But would you have done that without someone triggering you? If not, why are you letting *them* negatively influence *you*?

Being emotionally intelligent means we stay true to ourselves regardless of how someone else is treating us.

If you would not lash out in that manner based on the true you, why would you let someone else influence you to go there? It happens all the time because when emotions are high, we are more vulnerable to letting negativity influence our responses.

How I Conquered My Emotions: A Traveler's Story

I was walking through the airport on my way to a speaking engagement on the East Coast. Ironically, the topic of that speaking engagement was Emotional Intelligence. You want to build your emotional immunity.

I happened to walk by a woman just as she shouted to a gentleman who was standing on the other side of me.

"I have money for you," she yelled.

Because I was right in front of her as the words came out of her mouth, it was as if she was talking to me. I thought I was being funny and shot back a response:

"You do? Great! I'll take it!" I winked and let out a little chuckle. I kept walking.

She was *not* amused. In fact, she started yelling at me. Everyone started to stare.

"You shouldn't beg for money," she said. "You're a horrible person," she added.

At the moment, I felt myself getting flustered. The blood was rushing to my head, and I felt a combination of embarrassment and anger. If this had been a year prior, in all honesty, I would have probably shot back a snide comment like, "Get a grip." And I would have stewed on this all day long.

Instead, I could feel it had triggered me. I was aware of the response in my body. And with the tools that I have now, I was able to quickly regulate that anger.

I simply said, "I was just joking. Have a wonderful day."

The woman continued to yell at me as I advanced up the escalator. And at that moment, all I could think was that this interaction had not been about me. She must be having a rough day, and I certainly did not need to add to it. I chose not to let her words negatively influence my mood.

How Emotions Cost Me A Job

This is a cautionary tale about a job interview I had when I was about eighteen years old. I was interviewing for a job that my sister had just vacated. It is important to remind you that I spent a lot of time in my early days trying to follow in my sister's footsteps. She was smart, she knew what she wanted, and she followed the rules. I thought I needed to be like her. It took me a long time to realize we were going to take quite different paths in our lives. And that was okay.

Here I was, interviewing for *her* job, and the interview was moving along swimmingly. Until the dreaded question:

"Your sister has done a great job in this role; how do you think you'll be able to fill her shoes?"

I could feel the tears; they were coming. *My sister is awesome; how could I step into her shoes?* was racing through my mind.

I was telling myself to stop. Now was not the time. I was taught that you never cry in an interview. But I was spinning out of control. I had no answer to this question. Hell, I was questioning it myself.

Needless to say, I did not get the job.

That is a perfect example of a mini-tragedy about someone, yours truly, who not only was not self-aware but certainly did not know how to regulate emotions at the moment.

And the truth is, conquering our emotions is so much harder when we are in fake-it mode.

Evidence Supports Conquering Your Emotions

Emotional Intelligence predicts performance. In fact, according to TalentSmart, Emotional Intelligence is the strongest predictor of performance, explaining a full 58 percent of success in all types of jobs.[4]

Decades of research now points to Emotional Intelligence as the critical factor that sets star performers apart from the rest of the pack.

Do you think a star performer is more influential within their organization than a mediocre performer?

You bet your booty!

Consider these additional statistics from Inc.com:[5]

- **People with high Emotional Intelligence make, on average, $29,000 more per year than people with a low degree of Emotional Intelligence.**

- **People with average IQs with high EI outperform those with the highest IQs 70 percent of the time.**

I could write a whole book just on the statistics of why EI is so important. In a 2004 *Harvard Business*

Review article, Daniel Goleman, a renowned EI expert, wrote the following excerpt that sums it up beautifully:[6]

> I have found, however, that the most effective leaders are alike in one crucial way: They all have a high degree of what has come to be known as Emotional Intelligence. It is not that IQ and technical skills are irrelevant. They do matter, but mainly as "threshold capabilities"; that is, they are the entry-level requirements for executive positions. But my research, along with other recent studies, clearly shows that Emotional Intelligence is the sine qua non of leadership. Without it, a person can have the best training in the world, an incisive, analytical mind, and an endless supply of smart ideas, but he still won't make a great leader.

Leaders with high EI understand this. They have set aside their egos and worked hard to consciously develop skills in order to:

- make better decisions
- listen more openly without judging

- be willing to consider other points of view

- be naturally curious

- manage their reactions

- understand what they can and cannot control

This is where we build trust and become positively influential. It all ties together.

DARE TO BE INFLUENTIAL

CHAPTER 5:
Conquer Your Emotions

The good news is, EI can be developed. The bad news? Remember, in Chapter Four, when we talked about becoming uber self-aware? This is when it shows up. You must have that self-awareness to fully develop your EI.

Here are five best practices for conquering your emotions:

1. Identify your triggers. We all have emotions and our emotions are triggered by different events. The more we can recognize what triggers us, the easier it will be for us to manage those emotions.

2. Take pause. Once you know your triggers, you can recognize them bubbling to the surface. This is the time to take pause before you react. If you need to count to three in your head,

do it. The reactionary response is what gets you in trouble.

3. Deep breaths. Taking a few deep breaths will slow your heart rate and reduce stress. In fact, even the Navy SEALs have a breathing method to help them cope with stress. Simply inhale slowly, hold for a few seconds, and exhale slowly.

4. Practice empathy. What might the other person be going through that you do not know about? Try and put yourself in their shoes. It is extremely hard to lead people into greatness if you can't put yourself in other people's shoes.

5. Recognize, respect, and release the need to hold on to that emotion. This allows you to not dismiss the emotion but to take the steps necessary to fully work through and conquer the emotion.

CHAPTER 6

Kick The Yes-Men To The Curb

INVESTMENTS AND
FINANCIAL SERVICES

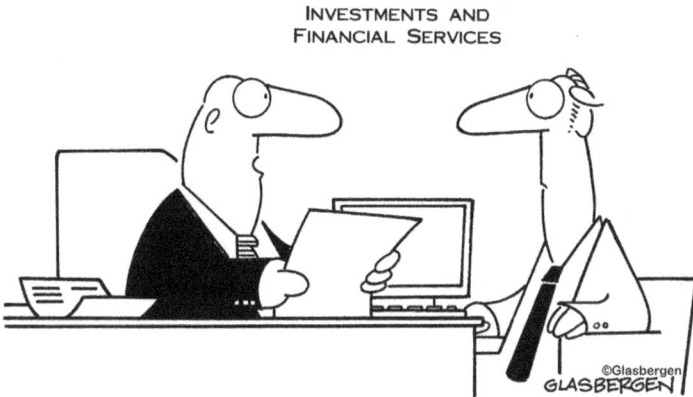

"The good news is, nobody will ever hate you for being rich."

The 1930s movie mogul Samuel Goldwyn of MGM famously said: "I don't want any yes-men around me. I want everybody to tell me the truth even if it costs them their job."

Are you willing to be radically honest?

The year was 1999. Mark Randolph, the then-CEO of Netflix, had to swallow his pride to do what was in the best interest of the company. This came about because his business partner, Reed Hastings, had the guts to have a hard conversation.

In his book, *That Will Never Work*, Randolph describes the moment when Hastings approached him to step down as CEO. While he would still keep the president title, losing the CEO title was certainly a blow to his ego.

Radical honesty and vulnerability were part of the Netflix culture, and both Hastings and Randolph lived and breathed those traits. Hastings demonstrated radical honesty when he made his case as to why he should take over as CEO.

Can you imagine all the feelings that come with that for Randolph? Embarrassment, ego, anger, the list can go on.

Randolph had to ask himself,

"Is what's best for me, what's also best for the company?"

He ultimately chose to step aside because he concluded it was the best thing for the company.

Had he not been more self-aware, he may have made a different decision. And Netflix may have been fine, but they likely would not have thrived.

This is what happens when you combine self-awareness with Emotional Intelligence. It's rare for people to reach this level of awareness. Would you be able to give up what's good for you for the betterment of the company?

Let that sink in.

You Cannot Afford Yes-Men

Yes-men can be detrimental to your success as an influential leader.

You will never be right about everything. In fact, we as individuals generally have fewer answers than we think we do. When we surround ourselves with people who will push and challenge us beyond what is immediately known to us, there is growth not only for ourselves but for everyone and everything around us.

According to Dictionary.com, a yes-man is a person who, regardless of actual attitude, always expresses agreement with his or her supervisor, superior, etc. For the purposes of this book, we will consider the term gender-neutral.

Ruthless honesty gets a bad rap. People are so afraid of hurting others' feelings that they avoid the direct truth. But how is that any better? How is telling someone a falsehood going to help them? It might spare their feelings in the short-term, but it does not even remotely help them with long-term success.

Brutal honesty can be and should be kind. You can absolutely be kindly direct. Just because you are going to tell someone the truth does not mean you have to do it in an antagonistic way.

As you begin to incorporate the advice in this book and grow your Emotional Intelligence, you will learn to keep your emotions in check while giving honest feedback. It is taking the emotional approach that gets us into trouble.

Fear prevents us from being open to experiencing and accepting brutal honesty from others. We fear hearing about our personal failures, or of being wrong, or perceived as weak. That is why so many leaders surround themselves with yes-men. Yes-men will tell us what we want to hear. They are agreeable. They do not rock the boat. If you want to stay in a comfort zone, then, by all means, surround yourself with yes-men.

For those of you looking to grow in your success and influence, you cannot afford to surround yourself with yes-men. It is essential to engage with people who will question things and will play devil's advocate. These interactions allow you to get the best results.

Look, the best decisions and successes are not always easy nor obvious.

Sometimes the journey is painful, but that does not mean it isn't exactly the right experience to enhance our personal growth as an influencer.

Why I Made The Boss Nervous

It was one of the most humbling moments of my career.

Mark, a partner and practice leader in the global consulting firm I worked for, was giving a PowerPoint presentation to the entire practice about the importance of having the right team of people around you.

He flashed a slide up onto the six-foot-wide screen.

"These are the people who make me nervous," said Mark.

And there it was—my name, right alongside some immensely powerful names.

My stomach lurched. How could I be part of this elite group?

"These are the people that make me nervous," said Mark. "These are the people I go to to push me out of my comfort zone. They don't tell me what I want to hear; they tell me what I need to hear."

He paused.

"And they make me a better leader."

Under Mark's leadership, that practice area exceeded growth expectations. In fact, the practice area enjoyed double-digit growth for five years in a row. A major part of their success occurred because Mark did not surround himself with yes-men.

There is an adage in business: half a truth is often a great lie.

Evidence For No Yes-Men

Being an influential leader does not always lend itself to being surrounded by people who will challenge you. As a subordinate, it can be scary to challenge the boss.

In a *Harvard Business Review* article (March–April 2017), Hal Gregersen writes, "As a CEO, your power and privilege leave you insulated—perhaps more than anyone else in the company—from information that might challenge your assumptions and allow you to perceive a looming threat or a new opportunity."[7]

The challenge with being insulated is it puts you in the position of being a lone ranger, making decisions based on the information that people weren't afraid to give you, combined with your level of experience and expertise. But the best successes build on the knowledge of others. As they say, two heads are better than one.

In this same article, Walt Bettinger, the CEO of Charles Schwab, called this dilemma his job's "number one challenge." As he explains, it takes two forms: "people telling you what they think you want to hear, and people being fearful to tell you things they believe you *don't* want to hear." Managers at all levels experience some form of this challenge, he points out, but "its grip is most intense in the top office."

As an influential leader, you must have those trusted advisors in place to tell you what you need to hear. If you are afraid of that, you are barking up the wrong tree to become an influencer.

DARE TO BE INFLUENTIAL

CHAPTER 6:
Kick the Yes-Men to the Curb

This can be a scary proposition because it is hard to be challenged. Our egos do not like it. It is one more skill we need to learn to develop to be our best influential selves.

Here is how you can develop that muscle:

1. Foster an environment of honest feedback and input from your most trusted team. If you cannot trust your team to have the company in their best interests, they probably shouldn't be on your team. Encourage your team to provide honest input, and do not berate those who share something that triggers you.

2. Exhibit an approachable attitude. Your team will be much more fearful if you are unapproachable, or if you show negative emotions when they are sharing their honest feedback. Providing that feedback and input

makes them vulnerable, especially as a subordinate. Do not give a reason for them to fear being honest.

3. Hire team members that have a strong balance of not being afraid to broach a difficult subject while not steamrolling over the organization. It is a fine line.

4. Hold honest innovation huddles. This is where the team can come and say anything without judgment. This helps the entire team build the muscle to ask hard questions in a respectful way and share thoughtful, honest responses.

5. Walk the talk. Ask the hard questions of others and demonstrate how it can be done respectfully. Don't just be a figurehead; talk to people at all levels of the organization because not only will they tell you things that you wouldn't know otherwise, it supports fostering the environment of honest feedback noted in item 1 (above).

CHAPTER 7

Ditch the Excuses

"I was ticketed for driving under the influence of neglectful parents, critical siblings, hostile teachers, and irresponsible peers."

Jessica and Bob ran a highly successful real estate business. They made a great team, and their clients loved them. But they were getting tired. Something was feeling heavy, and they could not figure out what to do about it.

Sitting in a conference room, we started to dig into what was going on in their business. We peeled back all their systems, processes, and client experiences. Our goal: to find efficiencies so they can free up more time. They just needed some space to breathe.

"What is your ultimate goal?" I asked.

Jessica answered, "I'd like to be able to take a vacation."

I continued down my line of questioning. "Why don't you take a vacation now?"

"We can't," they both answered. "We have to be available to our clients 24-7."

I went into a further line of questioning, pushing them to think beyond their current mindset, a set of beliefs common to many real estate professionals.

"Can you add a sales associate or hire a part-time assistant?"

"Can you return calls from vacation on a designated day or time of day?"

"Do you have a slow season? Can you schedule a vacation between closing dates or have a colleague attend in your place?"

For each question I asked, they had a rebuttal. They were afraid to miss the opportunity to take a new listing; they always attended the closing of their sales; who will do the final walk-through or troubleshoot last-minute issues with the banks? Potential buyers call them early in the morning and late at night—what if they miss a call because of cell phone reception? What if their clients feel abandoned and take their business elsewhere? They had fears that made them create excuses to cover every scenario.

As the conversation went on, as I offered a different perspective and potential solutions, I could see the lightbulb start to come on.

"These are normal challenges for independent contractors and small business owners. The good news is that all these obstacles are surmountable with thoughtful planning. You just have to make the decision to figure it out because everyone deserves a vacation to rest and recharge their batteries, especially in your business," I said.

It is was almost like I had to give them permission to make time for themselves.

Several years later, I met up with Jessica and Bob. They happily told me that they had made a point to take at least one vacation annually. They credit me for giving them the space to make it happen, simply by giving them permission. They have learned to work through their excuses and do something that ultimately makes them happier and better able to serve their buyers and sellers. They no longer feel on the brink of exhaustion; looking forward to a restful vacation (or two) helps them stay positive through the tough days.

The other win in this situation? They are showing up at a higher level as business and community leaders and their business has grown exponentially.

Funny how that happens when you give yourself permission to relax and allow yourself to enjoy a much-needed break.

Excuses Are The Silent Influence Killer

Each one of us has at least one story—big or small—that can stop us in our tracks: *We are too young, too old, too experienced, too green, too tired, too poor.* Every single person, at any moment in time, can find an excuse to stop something from happening.

The thing is, using those stories as excuses is going to hold you back as a leader.

Excuses do not inspire; using the same tired excuses weakens your ability to lead and stops you from becoming an influencer.

To be influential, there is no place for constant explanations around why something cannot happen. Your role as a leader is to figure out a way through *any* excuses that arise.

If you are using excuses to lead, you're not positively influencing the troops.

Let us take a look at why excuses arise. Excuses tend to show up for several key reasons:

1. We are avoiding doing something we do not want to do

2. We are afraid of something

3. We do not know what we want

4. Our old story serves us in some way

5. We are defending our behavior

As leaders, you get paid to make decisions that scare the bejeezus out of you. Just because you are making the hard decisions, or taking risks, does not mean you aren't scared. It means you are willing to push through and do it anyway. Sans excuses.

This is why successful leaders make the big bucks. Have you ever heard someone ask why top leaders make so much money? They are highly compensated because they are making hard decisions, eliminating excuses, and taking risks. They are doing the things that an exceedingly small number of people are willing to do. Most everyone else loses their focus because they rely on old, tired excuses rather than finding a more positive way to move forward.

---

*For every excuse you have,
someone else has a better one.*

Excuses live in the negative. They showcase why something should not be done. And they lead to quitting. But successful leaders focus on the positive. They know the only direction to move is forward. Successful leaders do not quit, and they do not make excuses.

If you are someone who wants to continue to make excuses, that is your prerogative. But if you are reading this book, it is because you want to be more influential. Being influential means taking hard action despite fear. So, buck up and move past the pesky excuses impeding your progress.

How I Learned To Ditch The Excuses

Steve and Tom, two key leaders of the Medicaid actuarial practice within a global consulting firm where I worked, were sitting in the lush boardroom of our Camelback offices, brainstorming on how to staff a new, highly visible multimillion-dollar project they had just closed. The staff was tapped; there were not a lot of resources available, and they couldn't hire fast enough. But Steve needed a strong project manager immediately, or he was going to fall flat on his face. And failing on a multimillion-dollar project was not an option.

They proceeded to peruse the internal phone list, from A to Z, looking for any potential staff members that had the time and skill for this project.

"Monica!" one of them blurted out.

"Yes, she'll be perfect!" Monica was, indeed, a strong project manager.

Off they went to approach Monica about working on this project. What they did not expect, however, is that she had all sorts of questions and excuses as to why this project wouldn't work for her. They walked away less than enthused and resumed the conversation by way of that phone list.

As they made their way to the Rs, Tom said to Steve, "Take Rehurek; she'll be great."

Steve did not know me from Adam. I could probably count the number of conversations I had had with him on one hand. He was hesitant, but he did not have another choice.

I had just gotten promoted into a new position as business development director. Not only was this the first time I led a department, but I was appointed to build this department from the ground up. It had not yet existed. I had a big task on my hands.

I was still learning my way around this consulting firm. I had a background in sales and marketing, but I was not yet sure I even knew what an actuary was. Heck, I had barely learned the difference between Medicaid and Medicare. To say I was not a technical subject matter expert was an understatement.

As I sat in my office working on the framework for this newly developed department, Steve came waltzing into my office.

He asked: "How do you feel about working on a client project?"

My initial thought was, *Is this guy crazy? What's the catch?* But without hesitating, I said, "Sounds good. What do I need to do?"

"Great. Meet me in Nashville, Tennessee, in two days," he said. "We'll have breakfast, and I'll fill you in."

Holy s***!

The next week was a whirlwind. Within thirty-six hours, I was on a plane from Arizona to Tennessee with little information on what I would be doing. I was scared to death. The next day, I tagged along to the governor's office, meeting with highly influential health policy and legal advisors, and trying to keep up with note-taking without even fully understanding what they were talking about. What I did not realize at the time is that this project would set the tone for what would be a huge jolt to my career.

To be honest, my "yes" was partially based on pure naivety. But I said yes because they asked, and I have always been one to embrace new opportunities. I was also always taught not to make excuses.

Now, I do not believe you have to walk blindly into situations like this. It might have been prudent for me to ask some questions. But if I had, I may not have taken that leap. And my career would look wildly different today.

That project put me on the map internally. I was seen as a go-getter; I was praised for my project management skills, both internally and externally, and I became an influential voice among leaders of the practice. To this day, some of those leaders are my clients.

Monica, however, lost out on a fantastic career opportunity because she was making excuses as to how it would disrupt her life. And it might not surprise you to know Monica has had an average career because fears and excuses held her back from growing her leadership potential.

Evidence Supports

We all have excuses that we can bring to the table, some more challenging than others. What we also have is the ability to choose to either let those excuses define us and disrupt our lives or be part of the fuel that propels us.

There are so many iconic success stories to showcase how people did not let excuses define them.

Richard Branson, the British entrepreneur and philanthropist, struggled in school and dropped out at age sixteen; he is now known to be worth approximately $4.3 billion.

Ben Carson, the first neurosurgeon to separate Siamese twins attached at the skull, was told he was stupid by his teachers.

Thomas Edison was told that he was "too stupid to learn anything." He was also fired from jobs for not being productive. And after many failed inventions, it has been told that it was his 1,001st invention that finally stuck.

What do they all have in common? Their innate resilience. The drive to make it happen against all the odds. They did not let their circumstances, other people, or their failures define them. Was it hard? Of course it was.

Hard should not stop you if you want it bad enough.

Hard is not a good excuse.

Margie Warrell, in a 2017 article in *Success* magazine, offers a great definition of excuses:[8]

"Excuses are really just masterfully engineered justifications we tell ourselves—and anyone else

in earshot—to rationalize our actions or, more often, our inaction."

When was the last time you made an excuse for inaction? Look, it is certainly human nature to a degree. What sets the hugely influential leaders apart is they have learned to push through that inaction and get things done under any circumstances. Plain and simple: there are no valid excuses.

DARE TO BE INFLUENTIAL

CHAPTER 7:
Ditch The Excuses

Excuses are influence killers. Positive, influential leaders do not make excuses. They make things happen. For some, this comes easy. Others must work hard to build this muscle.

If you are serious about being an influential leader, here are some steps you can take to eliminate excuses from your repertoire:

1. Know what you are working toward. When you know what you want, and you have your eye on that prize, you will not let anything get in your way. Make sure you are clear about what you are moving toward.

2. Understand what motivates you. We are all motivated by different things, but it is important to be in tune with what drives us into action. When you are motivated to move toward that goal, excuses won't stop you.

3. Get comfortable with fear. People assume successful leaders don't have fears. Quite the contrary. They feel the fear, and they bring it along for the ride. It is part of the excitement of leading.

4. Catch yourself in the act. If you find yourself avoiding things and then making excuses as to why you cannot move forward, stop yourself dead in your tracks. Awareness is one of our most powerful tools. The more aware you are, the better you will be able to start eliminating those excuses.

5. Figure out how to work through your fear. Leaders figure out how to step through fire even when they do not want to do it, even when they cannot see a safe path ahead. All you need to decide is what the next best step is, then take it and keep moving forward.

6. Rewrite the stories. Instead of letting yourself believe they are holding you back, determine how you can use those stories to propel you forward.

7. Let go of old stories. You may have stories from generations that are so ingrained in you that it is hard to move past them. Leave the past where it belongs.

CHAPTER 8

Quit Whining and Work Hard

"It's your *attitude*, not your *aptitude* that determines your *altitude*.
That's the philosophy that got me kicked out of pilot school."

Startling statistic: For every five companies that we work with at The RFP Success Company that say they want to win more business, only one is willing to do the work.

Zoe, CEO of a small multimillion-dollar healthcare company, came to us because they had been bidding on Requests for Proposals (RFPs) for many years with extraordinarily little success. This meant they were putting in hours and hours of hard work to continuously hear the word "no." It cost the company a lot of money and the business was in trouble. Zoe had the undeserved misfortune of not being able to bid on enough RFPs to justify having a full-time person dedicated to the effort.

Zoe's win percentage was relatively average, winning about three out of ten proposals. That was not enough. Without a dedicated proposal team, they were spending more money bidding than they were winning. They were losing even more money because they were pulling team members to respond to RFPs rather than servicing and building additional revenue streams with their current clients. Ultimately, the team was tired and frustrated.

"What do we need to do to double our win rate?" Zoe asked.

"It's not going to be easy," I said. "It requires a change in mindset, a change in culture, and a big shift in processes. You need to have a stronger up-front strategy and your team needs to build five days in on the back end so we can review the response and have time to make course corrections."

"That won't fly; my team doesn't have enough time to meet that schedule," said Zoe.

"You can either make the changes, or you need to be willing to accept the results you are achieving right now," I said.

I told Zoe the truth: It was going to be a lot of hard work, but they would reap the benefits if they were willing to do the work. After careful consideration, Zoe agreed to make the changes.

Making these changes was not easy. Our company was able to do an audit on past RFP responses, a complete assessment of their current processes, and come up with a game plan to help them submit winning bids. The team had to buy into new deadlines, new approaches, and they had to get comfortable being uncomfortable.

Most of them embraced it right out of the gate. The team was tired and frustrated, so they were certainly eager for change. And there is nothing worse when you are working hard and putting in the time, only to lose the business.

Sure, they had been working hard. But they needed to be working hard in a *different* way. Shifting their perspective, finding approaches that would resonate with the buyers, and creating time to develop winning bids was a lot of hard work. But they did it.

The following full year, they were able to win eight of their ten bids, an increase from 30 percent win rate to 80 percent win rate. They were thrilled.

Influence Requires Hard Work

The phrase *hard work* can be a bit controversial, so let us get some context out of the way.

If you want to be influential, you are going to have to work hard for it. This does not necessarily mean eighty-hour workweeks, killing yourself to the point of stress and fatigue. You can work *smart*, but you must put in the effort.

The goal is to become more efficient. Working smart opens the space to grow. You continue working hard, but it is now at a more efficient, value-added level. What you do not want to do is work hard and continue spinning on the tilt-a-whirl.

You will have to learn things that are uncomfortable. You will have to set aside your pride. You will have to take the initiative and be resourceful.

Unless you are willing to work hard and put away excuses, you are not going to get to the level of success and influence that you desire.

If you are someone who does not want to do what it takes, that's certainly your choice. Just know you will hit a ceiling with your success. You are probably not going to get to where you want to be. And let us face it, it is much easier to avoid the hard. Dealing with the hard is *hard*.

The difference is influential people define hard work differently. Working hard is a way of life for them. It does not feel heavy. It feels driven.

Again, working hard does not need to mean becoming a workaholic. Let us address the five keys to working hard that will lead to your success:

Doing what needs to get done, regardless of whether you *feel like* doing it. Working hard means you must push through to do the things that may not excite you. Sometimes—actually, many times—you have got to show up and clean the poop. The lower you are on the totem pole, the more poop you must scoop. At least until you get to the point where you are able to delegate, or as a business owner, you have more money and resources at your disposal to hire people to help.

Being resilient and pushing through when you get knocked on your patootie. When we talk about working hard, we are essentially talking about resilience. For each one of us, we have things that come easy, we have things that trip us up, and we have challenges and roadblocks in our lives that get in the way. If you want to be an influential leader, that resilience will see you through. When something knocks you down, you will get back up. The quicker you do, the better positioned you will be.

Making hard choices and hard decisions. As a successful and influential leader, you will have to make difficult choices and unpopular decisions. Decisions that you believe are best for the company, but not ones that everyone agrees with. People around you will complain, and they will judge you. Their fears and objections cannot derail your forward progress.

Doing the work to grow as a leader. If you want to be an influential leader, you must work at it. There is no magic fairy that will show up in the middle of the night and deem you influential. You have to deep dive into self-discovery. You must embrace continuous growth. You must check your ego at the coat check. And you certainly must get comfortable asking for help and trusting the people around you.

Developing skills to work smart. When we talk about hard work, we also mean *smart* work. Yes, sometimes that means hustle and grind. But again, this is not about working eighty hours a week and spinning your wheels. Working smart is about efficiency and effectiveness. You must learn to let go of control and become in tune with how to best use your time. You must be willing to take time to learn the skills of productivity and efficiency if you want to be more effective at what you do.

Why I Value Hard Work

It is not always easy to work hard. It is not always easy to accelerate over those speedbumps or push through the barriers. But hard work is required.

In 2013, I was diagnosed with Grave's Disease after many years of searching for a diagnosis. Let me just say, Grave's Disease sounds worse than it is. It is a pesky thyroid disorder, but it is not life-threatening or serious—just a pain in the patootie. Everyone has varying symptoms, but how it mostly presented in me was with severe fatigue and mental fog.

For the first few years after diagnosis, two sides of me showed up.

First, the side that was not pretty, which was the excuse side. There were things I said I could not do because of the symptoms I experienced. I pulled out many excuses because "I have thyroid issues." It is one of the reasons I am so passionate about eliminating excuses because those excuses didn't serve me at all.

On the other side of the coin was that side of me that was resilient. I pushed through and did hard things because I did not have a choice. What

I mean by not having a choice is that for what I wanted in my life, there was no other option. I had to keep working and building my business to get to the level of success that I desired.

During this ping-ponging from excuse-mode to mental fortitude, I was miraculously able to get a lot done. But I was still holding myself back. The disease had taken its toll on my health, and in addition to the fatigue and mental fog, I had also become grossly out of shape.

Enter my business coach team.

It was a big year for my business, but I was looking for more. I had audacious goals, so I hired a business coach duo to help with my strategy to get to my million-dollar year.

After mapping out the strategy that would get me to my goal, they asked me one simple question: "What is going to hold you back from reaching this goal?"

The first thing that came to my mind was, "Nothing!" After all, I was a workhorse; I could push through anything. I had proven it with my thyroid. I may be tired, but I was still kicking ass.

And then I thought, "What if it were better?" What if it were hard in a different way? And of course, that flashing neon sign with the word "Health" popped in my mind.

Yes, indeed, I would need to get a better grasp on my health.

Now that I had tied my health to my success, I was ready to go. I found my health coaches that specialize in thyroid and hormone issues, and I was well on my way to much better health. Within a few months, my bloodwork had drastically improved, and I felt a million times better. No more excuses that my thyroid would hold me back.

Even now, I occasionally slip and fall from not following those practices. It is my Achilles heel. It is *hard* for me to stay the course. I must be darn-near perfect with my eating, or I end up on the deep end of weight gain and fatigue. And for a foodie who adores rich, wonderful food, it bums me out. It is something I tangle with daily. Yet my choice is to continue that fight. Hard, yes; impossible, no.

What has come from this experience is that I now have a monthly practice of reviewing what is not working in supporting me in reaching my goals. I ask myself questions such as: "What's too hard? What isn't working? What could be better? and What would give me more fulfillment?" And then, I formulate a game plan for how I am going to fix it. It has become a great way to work through the issues holding me back. And all sorts of fun things have come out of this exercise.

Moral of the story: Sometimes, we must push through what is hard; or sometimes we just need to figure out how to make it easier.

Evidence Supports That Hard Work Leads To Success

Successful people do not wake up successful. They are not handed success. Even those that are handed a perfectly profitable company, a robust trust fund, or every opportunity in the world, will stumble if they do not know how to be successful. Just because you are handed an opportunity does not mean you will succeed. Just because you are handed money does not mean you will be influential. That is all a myth.

Think of legendary basketball star Michael Jordan. Sure, he was born with some amazing talent. But he had to work hard to get to the level that he has gotten to. You can say the same about iconic quarterback Tom Brady. Read anything about them, and you will learn how intense their routines were. For each of them, they had the unyielding desire to be the best there ever was. Do you think they could have done that without hard work? Um, no. The answer is no.

Mark Cuban, the self-made billionaire and owner of the Dallas Mavericks, is another great example. He hustled from a young age, learning all he could about business, and according to Investopedia.com, is worth an estimated $4.1 billion as of January 2020.

In a January 2019 Inc.com article, contributing editor Jeff Haden, shared Mark Cuban's Number One Thing that Separates Successful People From Everyone Else.[9]

According to Cuban: "It's not about money or connections. It's the willingness to outwork and outlearn everyone."

A further point that Haden makes in the article is it is about working hard, but also about working smart. It is about both.

If you are getting hung up on the phrase "work hard," then you need to eliminate that excuse. Because that is what it is. It is semantics. Successful, influential people do not get hung up on things like that because they know it is not a good use of their time. They also know it does not matter. They know they must work hard; they know they must work smart. They do the work to have the skills to make it happen. No excuses, no passing the buck, just straight-up ownership of their own destiny.

DARE TO BE INFLUENTIAL

CHAPTER 8:
Quit Whining And Work Hard

Moving past excuses and developing the fortitude to work hard is doable. Work through these six exercises to help keep you on track.

1. Work smarter. For each activity that you undertake, ask yourself how it is contributing to your ultimate goal. Ditch or delegate anything that is not in alignment.

2. Keep an excuse journal. For each excuse you find yourself making, write it down. Then go through the exercise of self-rebutting your own excuses—every single one of them.

3. Be resourceful. Learn how to tap into technology, people, and systems to make you a more efficient leader.

4. Focus on forward momentum. Be committed to personal and professional development.

5. Ask for help. You cannot do it alone. Influential leaders are willing to trust those around them and ask for help. Even if it stings.

6. Borrow my monthly practice of asking yourself what is working, what isn't working, and what could be better. Then solve for each of those.

CHAPTER 9

How To Sustain Being Influential

"Our motivational speaker cancelled.
He didn't feel like getting out of bed today."

In the popular book, *Chop Wood Carry Water*, author Joshua Medcalf tells a story of one boy's journey to achieve his lifelong goal of becoming a samurai warrior. In the chapter titled, "Uncomfortable Isn't A Choice," this boy's mentor tells him a story of the Navy SEALs:

> *Eighty percent of the men who enter SEAL training drop out, many because their bodies simply shut down. I met a SEAL once, and I asked him why they put themselves through such extreme circumstances. And I'll never forget what he told me: "Under pressure you don't rise to the occasion, you sink to the level of your training. That is why we train so hard."*[10]

While most of us are not Navy SEALs, at the end of the day, we still must train ourselves to build new habits. We must be willing to make that decision, to tell ourselves "yes" to developing the skill of being influential. Because when times get tough, we will sink to the level of training we have.

To what level are you willing to sink?

To maximize your influence, it is important that you discover your own genuine influencing path. Everything in this book is meant to help lead you to that discovery.

THE PATH TO INFLUENCE

Influence is not an event; it is a process and a journey. Your level of commitment will determine your ability to hone these skills and stick to the journey.

Have you ever been frustrated when a computer program or phone app updates and there are annoying changes that feel clunky and arduous? Facebook is one that comes to mind; they rearrange the Newsfeed, and it puts everyone in a tailspin. For days, there is significant commentary on posts about how annoying the new updates are. And then, within a few weeks: silence. Nothing but crickets.

That is because it has now become a habit, which is simply a behavior change. This is an example of a forced habit. We are forced to accept the changes, or we choose to walk away from using the application.

What is even more interesting is that many times, within just a few weeks, we can no longer envision how it used to be. We have now fully embraced the new format or habit.

It is your turn now to transform your habits and develop new behaviors using the action steps from each chapter. All of the chapters were designed to give you specific steps that you can work through in your quest to dare to be influential.

This will not happen overnight. We do not just wake up and decide we want to be an influencer, and so it is. There is work to be done, and it's a continuous journey.

When you begin to develop new behaviors, you may be tempted to quit because it feels unnatural. The change can be uncomfortable, but the payoff is worth it. I encourage you to make the commitment and stay the course to reap the reward of becoming an influential leader.

DARE TO BE INFLUENTIAL

CHAPTER 9:
How To Sustain Being Influential

Put on your patience hat, get excited about your future self, and begin to put new behaviors into place.

1. Prioritize each of the hidden secrets so you can focus on one at a time.

2. Tackle one action item at a time for at least twenty-one days. Avoid moving to the next action item until you have developed the subconscious habit.

3. Create a schedule to help keep you on track. Put it into your calendar, task app, or however else you track ongoing projects.

4. Anchor your habit to an existing embedded habit. An example of an embedded habit is brushing your teeth. An example of anchoring would be, "I am going to listen to one audiobook chapter while I brush my teeth."

5. Anticipate obstacles. When you get off course, do not fret because it will happen. The important thing is to pick up where you left off and keep going.

6. Develop accountability to keep you on track by using tools such as an accountability app, a partner, or a coach.

7. Reward achievements. When you find that you have established the new behavior, give yourself a small reward.

CHAPTER 10

The Future of Influence

"I wrote the book *'How To Guarantee Success Every Time'* but it was a flop."

What is the future of influence? Jacob Morgan, futurist and author, conducted a survey of 14,000 LinkedIn members that identifies the skills, mindsets, trends, and challenges that future leaders will need to adapt to over the next ten years.[11]

Not surprisingly, more than half (51 percent) of respondents said leaders would need to know how to be motivating, engaging, and inspiring.

While that may seem obvious, there is a significant lack of these attributes in leadership today. This fact is important to grasp because the expectation to exhibit these traits will be much higher in the future.

Studies indicate that three-quarters of the worldwide millennial workforce will leave their current positions because their managers do not nurture their potential to be leaders.[12] Because today's workforce wants to learn to be influential leaders themselves, you need to be prepared to teach them.

Throughout this book, you have examined the six hidden secrets to increasing your influence. You have been given action steps to take in each of these six areas:

1. Screw expectations

2. Know you, do you

3. Conquer your emotions

4. Kick the yes-men to the curb

5. Ditch the excuses

6. Quit whining and work hard

Now is the time to begin your journey and commitment to becoming an influential leader today and well into the future.

The ability to influence is not as straightforward as it once was. The continued rise of technology and artificial intelligence (AI) changes the way we lead. The 2020 pandemic has changed the way we connect. New generations expect authentic leadership and will not relate to anything else. The next generations expect opportunities to grow into authentic and influential leaders themselves, and they need mentors to guide them.

In a January 2020 article for LinkedIn[13], Deepak Bhagat, co-founder and COO at Applify, lists ten attributes that every 2020-and-beyond leader needs to have. Among those attributes: transparency, tech-savviness, and the ability to create more leaders. I would offer that the last one change to the ability to create more *effective* leaders. You will not be able to influence without these skills.

Understanding and keeping your fingers on the pulse of future trends is part of the job of an influential leader. Your workforce and followers expect to look to you for answers, ideas, and inspiration.

Let us look at a few of the future trends that will be essential for influential leaders to learn and master.

Technology And AI

No consideration of the future can ignore technology and artificial intelligence (AI). These two areas have grown at a dramatically accelerated pace in recent decades. Technology is rapid, it is adaptive, and influential leaders must do their part to keep up with it.

The challenge is it is hard to keep up. According to an article in TechJury.com, only 33 percent of consumers think they use a technology that features artificial intelligence, yet 77 percent use an AI-powered service.[14]

Baby boomers have watched as the futuristic tech toys from the 1960s cartoon "The Jetsons"—once merely fantasy—have become a reality. The use of technology for communication was already moving ahead at warped speed and has only increased with the 2020 pandemic.

BBC News reported online video conferencing giant Zoom sold its first shares to the public in 2019, with a value of $15.9 billion. As of early June 2020, that value had increased to $58 billion.[15]

In the 2002 Steven Spielberg sci-fi movie, *Minority Report*, many of the predictions of what would come to life by the year 2054 have already surfaced. Driverless cars, personalized ads, and voice-controlled homes seemed unrealistic at the time, but they are becoming, or have become our reality.

Technology is not going anywhere, and it's going to continue to develop at warped speed. There are so many benefits, but there are challenges as well. We see less intimacy in our human connections. Ironically, the new generations who have never been without technology are the ones craving more authentic interaction the most.

It will be the responsibility of influential leaders to create a way for their teams to feel connected amidst the rapidly changing technology world.

Continued Transparency

The newer generations desire authentic leadership. They are mission-driven and genuine, and they will not follow because of hierarchy.

In an Inc.com article dated January 2020, author Rhett Power points out that the new age of trust, honesty, and personal initiative has finally begun.[16] It is no longer merely lip service; it is reforming our reality. With that comes the responsibility for influential leaders to be more emotionally intelligent, more authentic, and more caring. You cannot be any of these things if you aren't implementing the six hidden secrets outlined in this book to take on the role of a positive influencer. The beauty of implementing the hidden secrets into your leadership style is that doing so will catapult you into that influential role. When you follow the action steps outlined in this book, you will be well-positioned to influence from an authentic and trustworthy space.

And In Closing

You are now armed with the six hidden secrets for maximizing your positive influence. Becoming influential is a journey and an evolution; it never stops. Is it hard? Sure. But that's part of the journey. When you are ready, that hard part does not feel heavy; it feels right.

I started my business about ten years ago. I'll be honest: the first five years were a struggle. While I felt closer to my calling, I was still searching. I was still a bit off balance.

It wasn't until about year six that I hit my stride. I finally embraced these six hidden secrets, and they set me free. I had certainly been learning about them throughout my entire journey, but now I felt rooted in them.

The benefits have been plentiful. There is much more confidence in my work because I know who I am. I feel closer to my sister now because I don't feel like I'm trying to be her. I am among the top less-than two percent of women business owners who have built a million-dollar business. And I feel well-equipped to share this message with you.

With influence comes a significant responsibility to use it for positive impact. If you genuinely embrace these six hidden secrets, your impact will be positive. But if you fake it, there may be negative consequences, both for yourself and for those around you.

Think for a moment about the weather—rain, wind, and fire can all be beautiful, but they can also all be wildly destructive. They can all destroy, and they can all create. Rain can cause mudslides, but also drench a drought; fire can destroy forests and warm our hands; wind can destroy homes, yet also create power.

We have a true lack of influential leaders—because when the hard kicks in, most people sign out. It takes a special individual to devote themselves to becoming a positive influence, but it is a high responsibility worthy of pursuit.

There has never been a better opportunity to step into the space of being an influential leader. The world needs you.

We all have the potential. Please do not settle for being comfortable and average. The world needs all the positive influencers it can get. I wish you good fortune on your journey.

ACKNOWLEDGMENTS

To all the positive influences in my life:

> My amazing parents

> My sister Lesli

> My nephew Daniel

> My brother-in-law Oscar

> My favorite mentor Steve

> The many wonderful bosses and other mentors I've had—too many to list

To all my friends who continue to believe in and support me

Cheri Fisher and Lesli Pintor for their input to make sure I was keeping it real

Henry DeVries and his team for helping make this book amazing

And, to all the negative influences in my life:

> Thank you for teaching me who and what I do *not* want to be.

ABOUT THE AUTHOR

Lisa Rehurek is the fearless (and ridiculously fun) founder and CEO of The RFP Success Company. Together with her team, she helps businesses win more business through Requests for Proposals (RFPs).

After a successful twenty-five-year career in corporate leadership positions, Lisa went out on her own to share her expertise and experience to improve RFP results for businesses of all sizes.

Lisa's achievements are vast, and she understands how to create systems and efficiencies that allow her to build and run a thriving business while achieving incredible results for her clients. She and her team have trained hundreds of business development staff and helped organizations win over $50 million in new business.

As an eight-time author, million-dollar business owner, national speaker/trainer, and podcast host, Rehurek is passionate about inspiring others to be the drivers of positive influence.

ENDNOTES

1   Gustave Razzetti, "Live Your Life for You, Not to
    Please Expectations." *Psychology Today,* Sussex
    Publishers, October 24, 2018. https://www.
    psychologytoday.com/us/blog/the-adaptive-
    mind/201810/live-your-life-you-not-please-
    expectations.

2   Peter Economy, "7 Highly Effective Habits to
    Become the Most Influential Person in the Room,"
    Inc.com., *Inc.*, September 3, 2015, https://www.inc.
    com/peter-economy/7-highly-effective-habits-to-
    become-the-most-influential-person-in-the-room.
    html.

3   Peter Economy, "Oprah Winfrey Reveals the Reason
    Millennials Really Frustrate Her (You Might Be
    Surprised)," Inc.com, *Inc.*, July 24, 2018, https://www.
    inc.com/peter-economy/oprah-reveals-her-biggest-
    frustration-with-young-people-you-might-be-
    surprised.html.

4   "About Emotional Intelligence", TalentSmart.
    com, Talent Smart, Accessed August 25, 2020,
    https://www.talentsmart.com/about/emotional-
    intelligence.php.

5   Travis Bradberry, "Why You Need Emotional
    Intelligence to Succeed," Inc.com, *Inc.*, March 12,
    2015, https://www.inc.com/travis-bradberry/why-

you-need-emotional-intelligence-to-succeed.
html.

6   Daniel Goleman, "What Makes a Leader?",
Harvard Business Review, January 2004, https://
hbr.org/2004/01/what-makes-a-leader.

7   Hal Gregersen, "Bursting the CEO Bubble",
Harvard Business Review, March/April 2017,
https://hbr.org/2017/03/bursting-the-ceo-bubble.

8   Margie Warrell, "Why It's Time to Stop Making
Excuses for What's Not Working", *Success,*
Success.com, December 8, 2017, https://www.
success.com/why-its-time-to-stop-making-
excuses-for-whats-not-working/.

9   Jeff Haden, "Mark Cuban Says 1 Thing Separates
Successful People From Everyone Else (and Will Make
All the Difference in Your Life)", Inc.com, *Inc.,* January
11, 2019, https://www.inc.com/jeff-haden/mark-
cuban-says-1-thing-separates-successful-people-
from-everyone-else-and-will-make-all-difference-
in-your-life.html.

10 Joshua Medcalf, *Chop Wood Carry Water*
(CreateSpace: 2015)

11 "New Research Shows How Leaders Should Be
Preparing for the Future of Work", LinkedIn.com,
January 16, 2020, https://news.linkedin.com/2020/
january/future-of-leadership.

12　"Summary of the Future Leader", getAbstract. com, Accessed August 28, 2020, https://www. getabstract.com/en/summary/the-future- leader/39212.

13　Deepak Bhagat, "The Future of Leadership: 2020 and Beyond", LinkedIn.com, January 12, 2020, https://www.linkedin.com/pulse/future-leadership- 2020-beyond-deepak-bhagat/.

14　 Nick G., "101 Artificial Intelligence Statistics (Updated for 2020)", techjury.net, July 4, 2020, https://techjury.net/blog/ai-statistics/#gref.

15　Natalie Sherman, "Zoom sees sales boom amid pandemic", bbc.com, *BBC*, June 2, 2020, https:// www.bbc.com/news/business-52884782.

16　Rhett Power, "4 New Trends in Leadership to Watch in 2020", Inc.com, *Inc.*, January 28, 2020, https://www.inc.com/rhett-power/4-newtrends-in- leadership-to-watch-in-2020.html.

www.ingramcontent.com/pod-product-compliance
Lightning Source LLC
Chambersburg PA
CBHW031942190326
41519CB00007B/625